Calm in the Dark

Cat Speranzini

Copyright © 2024 by Cat Speranzini.

All rights reserved. Printed in the United States of America. No part of this book may be used or reproduced in any form or by any means without written permission from the author except in the context of reviews.

Grey Coven Publishing
greycovenpublishing@gmail.com
Carver, MA 02330

www.greycovenpublishing.com

Cover by Melissa M. Combs
Instagram: @theenchantedpoetess

ISBN # 979-8-218-46255-0

DEDICATION

For the person I was, may she rest in peace. For the person I've become, may I love her as he never could.

For Tim—the one broke me and the one who patched me up again.

"the things of the night cannot be explained in the day, because they do not then exist, and the night can be a dreadful time for lonely people once their loneliness has started."

- ernest hemingway

Other Poetry Collections by Cat Speranzini

Tastes Like Goodbye

Watercolor Souls

content warning: this book contains mentions of depression, anxiety, self-harm, grief, and trauma.

Prelude (12/23)

She is as vengeful
as the wild undercurrents
of the fiercest sea,
a midnight maelstrom sending
sailors to the ocean floor.

cat speranzini

calm in the dark

Making the Bed

cat speranzini

i. introspection

If I had to pick my favorite place
I would say inside my mind
where I can replay memories
and fix any mistakes I find.

cat speranzini

The North Star Misleads me in the Dark

You take my trust and throw it
from the highest cliff, watch
it fall to the water below
then let it float, every action
a bid for control.

You touch my body, but never kiss
me on the lips because desire isn't
intimate and in the games with
lock and key, you play me
but not for keeps.

You leave me waiting for the proof,
make grand promises and never
follow through

because I am the void and you are the star,
only shining when I'm dark.

I should have left, this is my fault too,
holding your light like it's true north,
and finding myself lost in tangled thorns,
farther in the woods than I've ever gone
before.

Buried Alive

I dig up your memories
to bury myself with them.
This heaviness is the same
as a weighted blanket:

I am comforted by pressure.
My body is restricted
while my mind roams free.

I will claw my way out
when I am through
mourning my loss.

For now, I need the soil.

(For now I need the grief.)

Waves

The shower runs my memories
down the drain.

I watch you slip through the grates
more like moonlight through the trees

and I stay.

I want to be water, fluid
and calming. Like rivers,
like streams. Or the ocean
waves hitting the shore.

But if I am the ocean,
I am the tide.
Never reaching the moon,
but always moving for it.

Always keeping it in mind.

All this to say
I love you. I love you.

I never stopped,
not even when I pulled away.

Vampirical

Some people have
a sweet tooth for sadness,
rolling waves of blue crashing
through my mind, turning over
until the bottom and the top
collide and I am sinking
as I try to rise to the surface.
Despair is my guilty pleasure.
Who wouldn't love to live
in eternal pain?
Immortality is a warm gun
and my tears fill the chambers
with wet hot desolation.

Farewell

Our time was always clear skied,
the stars strung like faerie lights
swaying in the night.
We kissed with conviction
as if love was a choice,
not predestined fate.

I remember when the hurricane
reared its ugly head.
I saw the first strike of lightning
hit a low-hanging branch.
You swerved the car left
with terror in your eyes
and I sucked in a breath
I never fully expired.

I was blinded by the moon
whispering promises of
the sun rising despite
a storm-ridden horizon
when your terror turned
to doubt and your hand
slipped from my thigh.

I saw the exact moment
you decided moving on

calm in the dark

was better than lying.
Who is she, I asked,
and you shook your head "no,"
not that a name would change
what we already know.

Out of that car and back
on the streets,
I listened to the rain
hitting concrete.
Part of me was angry,
a part of me pained,
But above all else
I expected the break.

After a while,
I walked home in the rain
and now when it thunders,
I remember your name.

*(first published in glass gates publishing spring 2024
anthology)*

The Poem He'd Write About Me

She's sticky like spilled milk I meant to wipe up, but then forgot. She holds on for too long, so I have to work to rub her off. My arms ache from the cleanup, it's almost easier to let her stay stuck. She's in my inbox asking for more even when I tell her to fuck off, she keeps on demanding I talk. She's a chore, like laundry I put off for so long it's overtaking my room. I push the piles on the bed to the floor when I sleep, but it's impossible to ignore in the morning when I trip on my wrinkled jeans. I suppose she's okay, if you like that sort of thing. But never have I ever fallen in and out of love so quickly.

Silent Treatment

Purple pins drop
in the silence between couch cushions
and I fish for them with a lazy finger
like I know I'll never find them
in the depths of oblivion
and we might as well be at sea
in a boat crafted from desire
springing a leak and the silence
seeping up, up, up
over the boards onto our feet
and I'm grabbing a bucket,
I'm throwing the water back
into the ocean, but you haven't moved
and we're sinking too fast, so fast
I can't breathe, the silence is suffocating
me and I'm scared to open my mouth,
I'll choke and drown, so I sit
on the couch and wait for you
to speak.

Reveries

There's a version of you I hold
that's all curves.

Curved lips, crinkled eyes, easy laughter.
Round muscles, semicircle arms
engulfing me.

A version that exists. But rarely.
One that comes in between edges.

Sharp bones, missed meals, hungry eyes.
Low growls, dark fantasies, hard bites.
Points like peaks.

Hills, I see mere hills.
But there's a mountain.

And still, I climb.

End of the World Party

Cassandra saw the future, but was fated to be forever overlooked. She knew the outcome and still, no one listened to her.

I knew you'd be gone by my next birthday, I told you people always leave. And you laughed like the edge of a knife as you said not to be a self-fulfilling prophecy.

But Cassandra could not stop disaster, she could only speak the truth and it's a lonely world we live in when we walk it by ourselves.

Love In No Man's Land

What a feat to love me,
such a hard task, a regret,
at least that's what you said
when you left.

But you forget the moon bound nights
sitting around bonfires, smoke sticking
to our clothes, damp from practicing
Muay Thai until our bodies were
too bruised to fight anymore.
You forget the heat
of two entwined souls, the urgency
of time slipping by as our skin aged
before our eyes.
You forget forever existed
where your shoulder touched mine
as we struggled to stay
in separate space instead of combine
because your friend was across from us
in the lawn chair he bought
for trout fishing off the coast
with the boat he owned for oystering
when the autumn rolled in,
but it was summer then
and we lived on the edge of idleness.
The heat connected us like two aspects

of the same being.
We could stay in the forests of Maine,
we could camp eternally by the evergreens
while I laugh at your rendition
of an emo song from the early two thousands,
your guitar reverberating off cabins
until sleep descends
like ravenous wolves and
we collapse into each other
like an exploding star, our atoms
crushed by the gravitational pull
of attraction, so fierce and wild,
we might die if we don't
give in to desire.

Had you remembered,
you'd amend: what a feat
to find love in the trenches
of hopelessness.

Moon Time

I woke from sleep with blood dripping down my
legs like melted ice-cream. But my blood is not
sweet, more like a sour note to an otherwise
beautiful dream. And the sheets are stained with
original sin, I could laugh at the irony if I dared
look into it.

In my dreams, I am a dancer and you're my chosen
lead. I rewrite our history so the villain is not you,
but timing. The fates are kinder to us in my
fantasies. We learn all the steps and execute them
flawlessly.

When the moon is out, I slip into that world, where
love is the focus and everything else blurred, where
roses adorn our bed instead of thorns, where I wake
up to your breath on my cheek, our legs intertwined,
no hope of
unraveling.

Shipwrecked

We're taking on water
and you're jumping ship
but I was taught a true captain
goes down with it.
So while you're swimming
toward the shore
I'm waiting for the sea
to claim me once more.
Go ahead and tell
your fair weather friends
I was the albatross
who cursed this voyage.
But if I recall,
the albatross was fortunate
until someone decided
to murder it.

Time of Death: 07.07

My pen is infused with longing,
my body injected with your gaze—
Pale green eyes boring holes
where I pull out my guts
instead of stitching myself back up.
I miss you, that's all I have to say.
But I won't. I'll rip myself open
at my seams and I will spill
my blood onto the page
because I could scream missing
and it wouldn't begin to cover
the extent of the pain.
I am too big for my body lately.
I am too full of what I cannot explain.
I need a surgeon to remove the weight
or a pathologist to examine the remains.
I love you, that's all I have to say.
But I won't. I'll rip myself open
and show you what I mean.
Words cannot convey
the extent of the damage
when we parted ways.
And I still wish, I had hoped,
we could be saved.

calm in the dark

Bar Flies

You came with a warning label
that I ripped off without reading.
My dad told me I have bad taste
But I kept ordering the same drink,
kept sipping when it disgusted me.
Send it back, he'd advise,
order something new,
I'll even call the bartender over for you.
But I shook my head,
I was too stubborn, too determined
to get the most from a mistake
I spent so long making.
You decided halfway through
I wasn't the drink for you
and without hesitation,
sent me back for a new glass.
Must be nice never worrying
who you offend,
must be nice choosing again.
Send the drink back,
my dad says.

But daddy, I love him.

Colossal

The tip of the iceberg is a fraction
of the whole.

So many things that can sink a ship
hide below the sea.

Her graceful waves can turn fatal
with an undertow.

We were holding our breath
for so long

with our hair floating
on the surface

like the tip of something deadly.

She contains so many beasts,
countless undiscovered things,

but nothing quite as terrifying
as you and I treading water

side by side, so utterly misplaced.
We were a colossal mistake.

ii. introspection

Why can't I hit
as hard as I used to?
Shadow boxing my shadow self
isn't easy anymore.

I hope this message finds you well

I mean, I hope it finds you at all.

I hope you're the one reading my poetry
incognito.

I hope you're vain enough
to think it's about you.

I hope it knocks you out
and I hope when you come to

it's my rage filled emerald eyes
with the fiery freckles
that resuscitate you.

I hope I stop wondering
if any of this reaches
your corner of the web.

I hope you die
in my mind
and I hope I'm the one
who wields the knife.

I hope you haunt
someone else,

calm in the dark

that your arrow finds
a worthier mark

if there's one who deserves
the anger in your heart.

I hope I can turn the lights off
and be calm in the dark.

You Up?

I have a luna moth pinned and framed on my wall to study up close and examine how her wings fall, how her body rests. The messenger of life and death. There's a text I have to send, my phone a threat on the nightstand. I let it ring, let it blink, within arm's reach. The luna moth on the wall: an empty shell of something beautiful. And I, on the bed: a mirror image.

White Chip

I did everything right
for one day.
Like an addict,
I need to count them.
Commit to this.
This is a journey
and I have taken a single step.
They ask me
to rate my commitment
in therapy.
How serious am I about recovery?
Today is a ten.
Tomorrow might be a three.
Showing up tomorrow
could be a struggle.
I pray I show up anyway.
One day is a start,
sixty days a habit.
I will keep counting
until you're nothing
but history.

Haunting

Why shouldn't I haunt you
the way you haunt me?
Roam the halls of your mind
with ominous moaning
like an opera singer
without an audience
to please?

Why shouldn't my name
be everywhere you go,
so prevalent it lingers
like a light show
when your eyelids close?

I can be just near enough
to make you wonder
if you're losing your mind
hearing my voice
when I'm nowhere
in sight.

This Heart is Out of Order

I don't know what to do with all this love, a faucet
of feelings with the knob stuck, endlessly pouring,
has nowhere to go, fills the basin and drips to the
floor. You hold out your palms, cupped and ready
to catch it, but it slips through your fingers, there's
no way to hold this. It comes like a tidal wave of
emotion. The drain can't contain this volume of
liquid—I try to keep it all in, let it drown my veins
instead, let my love flow through my limbs until
I'm waterlogged and pruned up. Because once it
starts it won't stop and even a plant dies if you
water it too much. So, to avoid the whole mess, if
the faucet is broken, we won't let it run.

Heartstrings

I pay my dues in the way I walk, shoulders hunched
and eyes trained on toes treading over glass.

In the way I sing, breathy and quiet so the syllables
are lost to the wind and no one can hear the notes I
miss.

In the way I love, feral and desperate, biting to
break skin and dragging claws down unsuspecting
backs—I just need a foothold so I don't plummet to
my death.

In gripping on to what still tethers me to you: my
palms ripped open and rope burned. And I could let
go, I could stop paying for something I don't even
hold, but I want to know what's on the other end of
what pulls.

Talons

There's an owl keeping me up most nights,
his hoots hit my ears like a war drum.
My body is so prepped to run
in the aftermath of us.

If I could see through an owl's eyes,
I might dive for the mouse
with wings spread wide.

I might soar past the canopy of trees
to the dew-stained grass beneath
and grab the unfortunate
within reach.

Talons.
Sharp talons, like tiny daggers
poised to strike.

The Lovers Reversed

You'll never find someone
who gets you like I do—
Builds up the worst in you,
encourages the bad habits
that once were but intrusive
thoughts in you—
I brought your danger to life
and you ignited mine,
we were Bonnie and Clyde,
except, didn't they die?
Well, we did too, star-crossed and tired,
A Scorpio sun meets his moon
and expires
from the exhaustion of burning
at both ends,
the town was red and we painted it.
You'll never find someone
who gets you like I do—
No one will let you burn out
like an exploding star.
This new girl, I heard, she helped you
rise up, like a Phoenix from the dust
and I stood by the wreckage of us
ready to extinguish my spark
rather than pack up and
move on.

Tidal

I can forgive
all transgressions to a point.

But you toy with me
like you are the moon
and I the sea.

My tides ebb then flow
only with permission:

A prisoner
to your gravitational pull.

Metamorphosis

Earth sinks into me,
slowly hardens around skin.
Should I be reborn
make it with a battle axe
instead of these tattered wings.

Monster

I'm trying to figure out
what the hell I turned into.

(*Pretty sure it's you.*)

Shark in the Water

If you catch and release
the hook still leaves a mark,
the fish still bleeds.

Sharks swim miles
for an easy meal,
the boys have to eat.

You removed my hook,
I'm free.
But I bleed, oh how I bleed.

And the boys,
they eat.

Edge-runners

We were moon bound,
love wound, lucky to have found
our reflection in the other,
I will dream of you forever—
sleeping between stars together.
We were running into the fire,
you were holding onto my heart,
the kind of guy whose whole life is art—
the hero until he's outed
as a fraud in the dark.

Trauma Bond

The moon never shines
as bright as it did the day we met.
But my hair stands on end
at the nape of my neck,
my incisors protrude
and my claws extend.
I howl at the moon,
I beckon you to come
close again.

Why would you, though?
With my yellow eyes,
split down the middle, serpentine.
My tongue is forked,
I hiss a hello.
My body constricts,
my scales gleam green,
my fangs drip venom
to inject a vein.

I envy the stars
reflecting off waves.
With clouds rolling above
and sea churning below,
I swim through the ocean
at a breakneck pace.

calm in the dark

I have teeth like diamonds,
a nose that tracks blood,
I'm not afraid of anyone.

Did you leave because
I wasn't what you thought
or were you scared
of what I'm capable of?
The moon has been gone
since we last talked.
And my shape keeps shifting
like it can't decide
the right one.

I've been tracking you down
in all of my forms
but I can't find prey
when it's camouflaged.

cat speranzini

Overkill

I'm dragging this dead horse
to the reservoir…
as in: I'm dragging him
to where you are.

A dead horse won't drink
but I'll drag him there
because I can't let it rest
and I'm unimpressed
that all you did is
shoot it in the head

and withhold satisfaction
by ignoring my calls
and leaving my texts
on read.

Was it easier to fade into the mist
like a ghost in the wind?
Gone, no trace to track down,
no one to tell
"We used to be a pair,
not buried in the ground."

Sorry, I'm buried.
You float away,

calm in the dark

light as a feather,
and who do I complain to
about the weather,

this raincloud of rage
over my head like a halo
and you... I'll bet
it's always sunny
where you go.

So excuse me for saying
I'm tied to my anger
and waging war
with this horse
I've been dragging
all winter.

The spring is blooming
but my halo still thunders
so I'm bound to my unmade bed
and the one you made for us
and I refuse, I will not,
lay down and give up,

because I know I can't make
a dead horse drink, but
I sure as hell can bring him
to water.

cat speranzini

Lying in It

cat speranzini

iii. introspection

When I don't have a lover,
I have a new tattoo,
because I'm not happy
unless I'm hurt.

Playing the Victim

In the dark, I admit
I made my own bed
and I lied in it.

In the daytime, I play
the victim of your crimes
and it's not deceit

but it's not quite right.

Splitting

I don't even recognize myself in photographs these days, can't even last twelve hours without a panic attack these days. I'm tired all the time but my skin is alive these days. If I look up from my phone my mind is in overdrive these days. I need wine to find the will to survive these days. I never turn off the goddamn lights these days. I lie to myself all the time these days. I seem to be moon blind these days. I don't believe a single word I say these days. I keep thinking there must be another way these days. I wish I could fix my brain these days. But I'm tied to my mistakes until I die these days. And I don't know how to make it right these days. But I promised myself I'd try these days. What if I can't stop the cycle these days. I want to be the person I write these days. I'll never give up the fight these days. Who am I without a cause these days. Who knows if you'll see the girl I became these days. She's in a cage these days and I need the combination to set free her rage these days. She's stronger than I can explain these days. Don't underestimate me these days, I'll exceed all expectations these days. I have nothing to lose and everything to gain these days...

Don't Be

This is not personal, this is a war
and you have won the battle,
but I am adamant
that if you start a fight
you have to be ready
to commit.

I will not empty
my pain into a ditch
when I have a plan
for it.

It's not my fault
you started a fight
you can't finish.

Being human
means believing
in something,
not selling out
on the first offer
you get—

Where is your conviction?
Were you ever sorry
For the things you did?

calm in the dark

I have more strength
than your ego
lets you admit.

Rebirth

There is no sun in my sky.
The dark is embedded in my eyes,
present even in the light.
These shadows betray my poet's soul.
Torturous memories eclipse my mind
and I am on my knees begging
for reprieve, willing the world
to replace my eternal night
with eyes that catch daylight.

Quicksand

A part of me is trapped
in the sands of last summer
and I would go back to rescue her
if I thought she could be found.

I know I should move,
but I'm fooled into believing
if I keep my eyes shut
dreaming will lend me
the energy to rise up.

So here we are,
with you in the clouds
and me six feet under ground
wondering if I could
sink any deeper.

Enough is enough.
Did you ever love me?
I loved you so completely
I destroyed myself.

And I know you're laughing
from the pedestal I built,
only concerned about yourself
because victory is more important

than anything else.

You know I would deconstruct
this tower of doubt,
but if I had that power once
it's long gone now.

Anyway,
I'm writing to let you know
my bones ache and my face falls
and I can't look in your direction
without again looking down.

Doing Time

The sky hangs
over a vaulted ceiling,
so far from view I forget
how the stars shine,
how the moon dances
between the leaves
of birch trees,
how shadows
hang from shoulders
dragging me to soft soil,
toes digging into dirt,
the scent of dew forming
on stalks of grass,
cicadas singing
in the thicket.
The walls here
are strong and sturdy,
a prison I crafted
flawlessly.
I might never go free.
How things change,
one day I'm running
and the next I'm compelled
to lay down and do nothing.

The River

I have hit a fork in the road,
but no one knows.
Like Pocahontas,
I look for the compass
in the depths of my soul.
Slow and steady?
Or am I wont to embark
on a journey through rapids?
Do I need the spark
of danger to distract from
the repetition of settling?
But each time I choose unexpected,
I am left with a thrilling ending.
The rising action and the climax
are a waterfall of satisfaction
until the rocks at the bottom
remind me the resolution
will always be frightening
and the steady path
is the one more enticing.

A Necessary Evil

Everything is intentional.
There are no coincidences.
Even you, dark and villainous,
were meant to stick a branding
iron in my back and spur me
toward a greater purpose.

I keep that branding covered
but most have had a glimpse
of the name behind my teeth
going bump in the night.

And I think you were right:
this treacherous terrain
in the game of life is meant
to offer us an opportunity
that we can either use
or toss aside.

Keep Running

We tied a knot with a piece of string
and walked opposite paths
until it pulled taut.
We waited there, neither of us budged,
we kept on waiting
or so I thought.

You broke first and you broke free,
I stood still in disbelief.
He found me there, lost in the trees,
broken string still dangling.
He took my hand, lead me through
but my thoughts were always on you.

Why wasn't I the one you chose to keep?
Where was the hamartia I failed to see?
If I follow the string back to the canopy
would you still be gone or there waiting?

He takes the hanging rope
and unravels the loose ends,
lets it drop between our feet
until I too am finally freed.
On the other side of being tied,
I look at this with brand new eyes,

calm in the dark

see rope burns traced
around my wrists and wonder
if, while tugging at the bit,
I pulled so hard the rope frayed and split.

The Cut That Never Closes

Sometimes I PROD at wounds / to see how much they've healed. / My fingers tug at jagged skin / pull off pieces of scab that dare / form over lacerated dermis / and force the wet, hot lesion open / so blood pools around my nails / and DRIPS down my limbs / until hitting linoleum. / This is called remembering / where I test how big the gash used to be, / where I check the size of the knife you used to slice / open my flesh and leave me / bleeding on my back. / Where I time travel to stare / up at the stars and DEFY / death, long enough to witness / the sun rising over the Atlantic. / Where I dip my toes / in the icy water of your influence / and I mourn all the nights spent waiting / for you to find me bleeding / in the sand. / Dried blood darkens my nail beds. / I pick at the cells, rub them off / so they're gone—as you are—then / restart the process of RIPPING apart / progress. / This is my favorite type of hurt. / I want the pain to pound my bones, / to know what I was fighting for, / lose the thing I loved most / a couple times more / so there is cemented certainty. / I am never going to make it / from beaten down / to CURED.

Stitches

I have been ripped open,
organs removed and replaced,
then stitched up again.

The body still functions,
but nothing is the same
and my abdomen
is fit for Halloween.

Recovery is a process,
every day a blessing.
I'm trying not to dwell
on what I lost

but focus
on what I gained.

Gentle

He hates when I hit,
says pain is just pain,
there's not pleasure in it.

My jaw clenches
to hold back a bite
and I want to scream,

I want to fight.

But he is not you,
he doesn't play
to win

and I don't know
what to do with this.

Selkie

Why shouldn't I shed my skin
when it no longer fits?
Shift my shape and change
my name,
live countless lives
with a dozen stories to claim,
write and rewrite, ride the waves.
I have a selkie heart
that cannot be tamed.

Dreams / Nightmares

I have this recurring dream
where you come back
and I let you—
Where I'm taking steps
like it's the first time I've ever walked,
where I'm falling in love like I've never
been hurt.
It ends much the same as it did
when you left:
I chase you and you disappear
slowly then all at once
and I look around, wondering
what I was running to
or from.

The Kraken

Legendary creatures
don't buy you dinner.
They crack ships in two
and pull them under.
Mysterious beasts
don't hold your hand
while you drown.
They swim away
and find another ship
to take down.
The lesson is,
if a monster attacks,
you shouldn't tread water
and wait for him
to come back.

cat speranzini

iv. introspection

Maybe I should stop screaming
his name.
If he paused and caught my gaze
I wouldn't know what to say.

cat speranzini

A Woman's Touch

Let me suture his wounds,
give him an EKG, monitor
the rhythm of his heart
until he's good to be discharged.

Don't ask me how my own heart
breaks and continues on.
Don't ask me to sew myself shut,
I'll keep opening back up.

I can fix him, that's a simple task,
his breaks are small, clean cracks.
Mine are spiderwebbed in porcelain,
no chance of being whole again.

Don't tell me he's the reason
I'm losing all feeling in my limbs,
the reason I can't trust anyone
or learn to love again.

I won't believe he's the one
draining all my blood,
freezing me to the bone
while I work to fill his cup.

My cup is empty

calm in the dark

in my hypothermic hands.
I'm too tired to get up,
too weak to try and stand.

At least I saved someone,
I tell myself, at least he's better
than before. I fixed him, I did that,
but now I'm bruised and sore.

I told you I could fix him,
like I have a medical license.
Did I not insist I could save
any broken man?

(Really, I can.)

Six Word Story

Love, like treading water. Don't *drown.*

Revisiting the Past

Imagine him gone before
he goes.
Imagine him dating her before
he does.
Imagine him...
No, you can't
bear to think of him
anywhere but here,
with you. Here, at a bar
bickering over some silly
misunderstanding,
melting together,
kissing too fervently
it disrupts
the acoustic guitar.
And he'll order another drink
and you'll pay, don't you always?
Ask yourself why you want
to be belittled before
you're FUCKED.
He's leaving, you know he's leaving.
He has one foot around your ankle
and the other out the door.
They all go.
But, not yet, please,
you beg.

cat speranzini

Just another hour,
Another day.
*Don't leave me today, I can't
do this today.*
Those words, say them
over and over and over
until every day has passed.
Until one of you
is dead.

Loose Ends

The horseshoe crabs mate in May.
They crowd the bay
so it's more crab than human.
I watch them every year,
Prehistoric artillery crustaceans.
So out of place
amongst the sand and waves.
I imagine this is how the world ends:
Cockroaches and horseshoe crabs.
I imagine this is how we meet again.
With me on the beach
and you in your truck
out on the street
looking at one another
as I punctuate the last line
of our completed story
and you drive off
into a new one.

Twin Flame

They say twin flames
can only be lessons,
not final destinations.

Their eyes are a mirror
so you can witness
how your actions
hurt others

but I hope to god
I'm not the monster
I saw in him.

He was an undercurrent

and I want to be
softer than the sea.

Gaslight

Rope burns hurt more
than movies let on.
Walking away from explosions
isn't so calm.
Drowning has never been peaceful,
poison isn't the easy way out.
Mind games don't feel clever
when your life falls apart.
It's hard to let go of something
that broke your heart.
I know, I've been where you are.
The first step is moving
into a new start.
A leap of faith can be freeing
if you trust the process
of healing—
turn it into art.

cat speranzini

Cool Girl

After Ashley Frangipane

When I was the cool girl
I was the complaisant girl,
the calm girl, the nonchalant girl,
the anything goes as long as we're fine girl.
The sex appeal is dripping from
my loose tongue girl, because it can trace circles
that'll blow your mind girl.
Look up at the stars girl.
Sing dirges in the dark girl.
Commitment is a crime girl,
he's better for just one night girl.
Never speak my mind if I want him
to stay by my side girl.
Listen harder than I talk girl.
Men are in charge and I'm scared
for my life girl.
The world plays in black and white girl.
Starve to keep them in line girl,
make them hungry for my mouth girl,
Don't think about why he keeps me around girl.
Troubled pasts are all the rage girl,
they're why I have these open legs girl.
My body is my claim to fame girl.
All they see is a pretty face girl.
The never gonna forget me

calm in the dark

for the rest of his life girl, the catalyst
not the trophy wife girl, the leave me
once he's had a good time girl.
the lusted after never loved girl.
"Hey, remember that cool girl?"

Lost at Sea

Grief is not a feather
it's an ocean.

There's a boat
in the Atlantic
that ebbs and flows
in taciturn waters.

There's a girl
with her knees
up to her chest
and she's rocking
with the waves.

There's a boy
on the shore
sipping bloody
marys. Not
thinking of her.

There's an island
called Hope
somewhere.
She's not sure
where,

calm in the dark

but she knows
grief can't last
forever. That
one day, Hope
will be the moor.

Do it Anyway

There are days I do it with a pain in my chest,
days I fight through labored breaths,
days I'm not sure will ever end,
days I never want to live again.
There are days I cry until my eyes swell shut,
days I drag my feet through the mud.
I've done it dirty and I've done it afraid,
I've done it without a cent to my name.
There are days I wish I was stronger,
days I'm proud of myself for trying harder.
I've fallen nine times, gotten up ten.
I've been red handed, guilty as sin.
But I scream, I claw, I do it when I can't.
I never claimed to be an innocent.
There are days I run across the field of battle,
days every word from my mouth
is like a death-rattle.
I can do it tired, I can do it falling apart,
watch me do it with a broken heart.

Innocent Until Proven

It's all eggshells and thin ice,
like I'm a hand grenade with no time
to find cover from the impending
explosion in my mind—
I've always been the girl on the run,
how did I become the terrifying one
who borrows hearts and returns them
broken, I have no regard
for anyone.
It's all shattered glass and 911,
like I'm an emergency with no time
to call an ambulance.
He came for me and I wrecked
all we had become
so he was forced to
leave me screaming
"I'm the victim
of villainous intent,
feel bad for the innocent."

Sheep in Wolf's Clothing

I'm somewhere between
the fiercest of creatures
and the lonely, the meek,
a weakling
who can't take out the sheep,
because I am half wolf
and half prey,
my claws not as convincing
as the tongue behind sharp teeth,
mostly howl and not much bite,
intimidating yet soft inside.

I Am Not

I am not made for longevity,
I am made to be used and thrown away.
I am made to be consumed by flames,
I do not burn and regenerate.
You'll fall in love in an instant
and discard me that same day.
I am not made to be a keepsake,
I am a candle, a brocade, a hazard,
a mistake.
I am a good time at best and a regret
if you let me stay.
I am not made with a lifetime warranty,
I am a catalyst, a match, crackling rain,
disposable in every way.
I am not a soulmate,
I am a wild animal in a cage
planning my escape.

The Sins of Man in a Bar on a Monday

The Atlantic was frigid today,
but the air is getting warmer,
the wind a mellow breeze
and when I stood in the water
with my hair blowing freely
I was reminded of the duality in nature,
how opposites exist as a balancing technique:
You sitting at the bar with a grin like
a cheshire cat who spotted his prey.
Me, standing strong and steady anyway,
how a rubber band is pulled and snaps
back with twice the ferocity.
How tonight is a threat
and tomorrow a possibility.

Writing an Ending

I'm not stronger because I survived this,
but I am smarter.

The man I loved was a character I created.
He came from me. None of it was real.
None.

I loved what I gave.

There are songs he introduced me to, movies, and
phrases. These are pieces I plan to save.

But there is no him. There is only the stranger
I shared a bed with.

I'm worth more than this.

To the man I created and invested so much in:

Two things are true.
I will always love you.
And I loved myself enough to leave.

How to Exist

The cicadas slept for thirteen years
waiting under the soil like flowers
not yet ready to bloom.
When the weather warms the dirt
they'll spring forth like
a cloud against the sky.

Fearless.

Fearsome.

Millions of them.

I am only one person,
but I know how to scream.
I know how to fight.
I know how to find another
and form a cloud against
the oppressive sky.

calm in the dark

Getting Back Up

cat speranzini

v. introspection

We catch the fallen stars
in our palms like fireflies
and hold them as flashlights
against the night sky.

Love at Second Sight

When I saw you, I knew
our lives were meant to
twist and tangle.
That I might not love you
right now,
but I'd find you later
and we would tie ourselves
with string
like a present forgotten
in the attic—
a pleasant surprise,
a perfect prospect—
and we'd dust off
our story
to finish telling it
when we met
in medias res.

Spilling Over

Sunday spreads her slow wings beneath my head
beckoning me to stop expecting and simply be—
Dusk shrouds the remnants of day in dark shadows
as the rain pounds harmonies on slippery concrete.
I want to be immersed in the sweet FA of sleep
But I cannot disregard the rhythm of raindrops
hammering his memory into my mind
and I am

in love with the cushiony pillow of his lips
like this rainstorm is the first time we've ever
kissed.

Lightning in a Bottle

I don't know what I did to deserve you.

They say you're more likely to get struck
by lightning than attacked by a shark.
They say lightning doesn't usually
strike twice.

I must be an anomaly,
I must be so lucky.

I had my share of sharks. I had my share
of lightning.

They say the only way out is through
but they never tell you what's on the
other side.

I walked through hell,
I survived.

And on the other side,
I found *you*.

The Second Day

Your eyes storm,
your voice cracks
the ground in half —
your face flushes
red: a sunset.
I marvel at the sky
beneath your skin.

Eclipse

Here, stuck in between
the first eclipse and the next,
we are dressed to kill

two birds with one stone.
Standing strong, we've learned
nothing will grow tall

unless we water
every last petal of it.
Bound by the moonbeams,

foolish to believe
there is light in the darkness—
hoping regardless.

(first published in Fuckus the Mag's 2024 summer anthology)

calm in the dark

Savage

I thought I was strong,
but I am sabotage incarnate.
When I stand up for myself,
I am really standing
against you
as you try to hold me
against you
and I rage, rage
against the death
of light.
I rage against
myself,
with you caught
in the crossfire.
You take the blows,
shield me.
When it's over,
I am all apologies.
Can sorry erase
the savage
inside of me?

Opposites Attract

Let's not pretend to be something
we're not.

I am a bird on fire and
you're running water, a river of promise.

Ever changing, flowing and raging,
yet calm. Yet strong. Someone to count on.

I cannot meet that energy. Because I know
what it is to burn—I know what it is to
fan the flames.

My wings leave a trail of ash
and your water leaves a trail
of smooth stone—

We could find a balance between
fierce and controlled.

Tension

Our bedroom is a mess
of sharp words and silent
treatments.
The sheets disheveled, the door
slammed then locked
with a threatening click.
I storm down the stairs
into the living room
where red wine splashes
out from the glass
and stains the floorboards
like blood.
I am tired of us
flip flopping from intimacy
to confrontation.
Is there no in between
of loving support—
my head on your chest,
no hand around my neck?
Or are we doomed to stain
the floors of this house
with chaotic conflict
talking in circles,
throwing stones
at one another
and missing the point

cat speranzini

as we dance around it
thinking our opinion
is the only one
that makes sense.
But as I look
at this wine stain
from one angle
it's shaped like a nine
and the other, a six.

How To Hold Me

Like a desperate howl at the ripening moon, like a
cherry stem tied, like I was gone too soon. Like tree
sap stuck in the crease of your palm, like the
impossible dark before a brand new dawn. Like the
pit of a peach abandoned on the side of the road,
like a dive in the ocean without any clothes. Like
damp hair drying in the mid-summer heat, like
pollen stuck to the hollows of your cheeks. Like the
first stalk of lavender, like a flower that hasn't
bloomed. Like a snake wrapped around your neck,
like the goddess of life and death. Like you love me
and you don't want to leave me just yet.

If People Were Rain

My kisses fall on whiskey lips, poison
I savor with a brush of my tongue,
thinking if people are liquid
you are cough syrup
and I am runoff.

You're in my bloodstream,
making my head spin, and I am
dizzy with desiring your
breath on my cheek.

But I am surface level,
no way to deeply penetrate,
just a shallow pool of
tepid water

pretending to be
a lake.

Talking to Ghosts

In the dark pools of your eyes, I swear
I see his shadow. Moving through walls
like a ghost, untouchable

and when we fight, it's not your name I yell,
it's his syllables pressed against my teeth
going bump in the night as I scream
and I scream and I
scream.

I know this isn't your fault, this isn't
anyone's fault. He haunts me
and I let him.

He hurt me

and I *let him.*

Tell me Something Awful
After Taylor Swift

Quick, quick,
like every second is a second too late
and we're chasing something
that's no more than a myth.
Tell me all your sins,
all you'll ever be
is a settlement
for injuries sustained
from past lovers who kept me caged.
You see, I was once a catch—
the whitest dove, in search
of an island in the middle
of the open sea, the sun shining
down on my unmarred wings.
Now I'm scared of too much
space, I almost prefer the
gilded cage.
I know better than to say
I hate the person I became,
the one who lies to save her face.
Quick, quick,
like there's still a chance
to redeem ourselves, with
armor and weapons, slaying
the dragons of deceit

calm in the dark

and living happily ever after
in our shared fantasies.

How Different am I *Really*?

My tongue is twisted like brambled thorns
when I touch harsh words to its tip,
and is the tip too much? Just the tip,
you insist, doesn't count. It's only
one part of a whole and I am greater
than the sum of the parts that make me,
greater than the parts that break me.

How different am I *really*?

All bloody fingernails, all bite marks and broken
promises. Till death do us part, but you're still
breathing and I dangle from the loose string
on the seam of your designer jeans as you
pull them up and leave me bleeding
on the mattress, pressing crimson
fingerprints into white cotton sheets.

Radical Acceptance

I hold it in my chest, the tightening
an embrace incubating my hate.
Anger is a secondary emotion,
but I can't tell what came first,
the chicken or the egg—
a cyclical debate that has me
spiraling through space.

I don't want to be mad.
I don't want to be mean.

I don't want to hurt the people
who matter the most to me.

Please, make it stop, I beg the world
to quit spinning. Please, make it stop,
I'll do almost anything.

And it does, it stops, with a cold shower
and a panic attack

listening to water droplets hit the porcelain bath
like a syncopated drumbeat and my heart
engages in a battle of the bands until my thunderous
pulse renders my eardrums ringing.

Please, just stop. Please, I can't breathe.
How is it fair that every second is a struggle
that no one else perceives—just me.

Only me. On the bathroom floor taking
quick and shallow breaths, my lungs
collapsing and every moment a threat
of something worse than death, slipping
between anger and anxiety as I fight
for control of this traitorous mind—
I just want to get better this time.

calm in the dark

The Poem He'd Write About Me pt. II

We have to talk. About the rage loaded and aimed
then recoiling in your chest. About the bathroom
light you keep on when you sleep because you're
afraid of the monsters you've never seen—the
monsters clawing beneath your ribs, in places that
won't allow the light to seep in. About the scream
trapped within your throat, how you release it from
your mouth to the walls of our room. About how
my ears are ringing and my fingers permanently
pressing them closed. We have to talk about your
savagery, the shadows that overtake your mind and
sink from brain tissue to carpet. About how I am
trapped, I am *trapped*, I love you but let me leave
the waters of your grief. I'll throw you a raft from
the boat, but you can no longer push me under in
order to float.

cat speranzini

vi. introspection

Grief is not a feather,
but it is also not a line.
His initials are etched on my cheek,
like my heart pinned to my sleeve.

Headfirst

The stars shiver when they hear your name,
like electric currents or undertows.

The moon shakes when you walk in the room,
like sun storms or black holes.

The cosmos tremble in your wake,
your chaos is widely known.

And I should move. I should go.

But you're an undiscovered planet
with rings for halos,

your gravity is unlike any force
I've ever known.

Inherited Rage

Cue the hurricane:
I am prone to birthing storms.
Lightning cracked skies
rough thunder roaring above,
rainclouds resting in my eyes.

My Body is a Knife

My arms can reach the full length of my spine
which I've heard can be a sign
of joint disease, just another thing
I inherited from a mother I've never seen.
And this body is foreign to me, it bruises
like an overripe banana. It expands
like a sponge, it stretches
like a rubber band. I am an alien
in a world of beauty queens.
The hairs on my navel are rough
like a kiwi. My wrists jut out
like thorns from the stem
of my rosy arms, my body pulls too pink,
a sunset of reckoning, the spider veins
decorating my Achilles' tendon
like paint on old canvas, and I study
the hollows of my sun spotted cheeks
and trace the jumbled mess
of fibrous tissue adorning my thighs,
wondering why so many mistake scars
for stretch marks, call them tiger stripes,
when I see this body as a knife—
bones and muscle encased
in rage, a primal *scream*
waiting to escape.

calm in the dark

Retrograde

The witching hour wakes me every single night,
like you're calling me from the depths of sleep and
wrapping your arms around my body.
I feel your warmth on my back, my chest,
looping around my stomach. You smell like
mountains and morning dew, like dirt
and musk. I wonder if you catch my scent
in the confines of your room. Always
separate, something written in the stars
keeping us apart. But still I reach,
and reach, I reach for you.

My arms extend, my fingers stretch, and if
I concentrate on grazing your fingertips
from miles away I swear I can feel the
heartbeats in your chest.

All these months mean fuck all when
it's your voice that rouses me like an alarm.
My bed is cold, but I cling to phantom warmth.
Can you hear me whisper your name with all these
towns between us? Do you dance with the ghosts
of what could have been us? I drift back to sleep
and keep you in my dreams thinking if my path
ever curves and lands me back at your side
I'll have enough sense to stay there this time.

What Color is a Thing that Leaves You?

The sky is not always blue, sometimes it's grey. I am not always sure, sometimes I hesitate. I think back to the night I handed you a bouquet and you stared blankly at my outstretched fist like you expected a punch rather than daylilies. Purple, like your favorite shirt. Purple, like the dress I wore on our last date. Purple, like a bruise. "Take them," I insist, but I mean all of me. And you take them, but you mean only for today. I beam at you like forever has lilac hues. You drop the flowers on the table like leaving and I am slowly realizing sometimes forever is grey too.

Oceans

Sweetness, do you believe—

the wind blows when you're gone.
Does it know what we misplaced,
collectively lost?

It must not, it must not
because knowing is a sob stuck
down in my lungs, a wet gasp,
a moist cough, one I can't
dislodge.

Sweetness, do you believe—

this flickering flame that ends
the world in fire and ice, blue
like the ocean—an immeasurable
pain.

How deep does it dive?
No one can sink that far and
survive.

Rough All Over

Do we see the same stars
rising over the sea, holding space
like a bird's outstretched wings?
Do we sing the same song
at exactly the same time?
Do we tap out the beat
with our hand smacking
our thigh? Can you taste the
syllables of my name on your tongue
when you hear someone else say it,
like a phantom limb you can't shake,
like pins and needles in a useless
leg? Do you gaze at the clouds moving
over the same damn horizon, do you know
we share a sunset? Do you bother to
watch it?

I am not always
After Kristina Mahr

strong enough to forget about
your whiskey lips / and little
white lies / your empty promises
and your hollow-eyed / smile, your
carnal desires / the bites like birth
marks / a baptismal rite that remade
my life / into something both holy and
horrible, / forgetting eludes me like a rip /
in the fabric that makes me / an ache
I am not always able to think around.

You're gone and I'm not sure I want
your absence to be something I

live around.

Bad. Again

My grief grabs hold and doesn't let go,
sinks its claws into the cavities of my ribs,
asks me how much longer I can hold my breath
before my vision fades to black and

I don't know, how would I *know*

how deep I can sink before I begin
to float?

And don't we all lose what we once
held close,

don't we all give up when we run out
of hope?

A little longer, I can keep going,
and my grief smiles like death
as I aimlessly kick, unsure

if I'm headed deeper
into darkness or if I'm close
to breaking the surface.

calm in the dark

Beached

A whale washed up on the shore last summer
and they closed the whole beach, sent out
camera crews and NOAA Fisheries,
and all I could think about was
the whale watching cruise
we used to take every
September

and how the last time we went
we didn't see any whales,
the ocean was secretive
and thoroughly silent.

But that first time?

There were dozens near our boat
and their calls were so breathtaking
I couldn't stop myself from crying.
I didn't visit the coast for a year after
she died, was so mad at the sand for killing
that gentle giant. And was she aware of her fate
as it unfolded or were her last breaths taken
in utter confusion?

Did she decide which way to go,
like Icarus' flight too close to the sun

cat speranzini

or Pandora opening the lid of the box?
Or was she off-course and afraid, separated
from her mate, so turned around that she got lost
in the waves and by the time she realized
what had happened it was already
too late.

My Religion

I am holding this knife over flesh
like it has answers for questions I don't
know how to ask, but I can't understand
what I hope to find under my skin, what
secrets my muscles and bones keep
from my shaking hands. The metal is cold
against the crux of my wrist and I tighten
my grip on its handle like my devotion
is a prayer at the altar of loneliness, like
god has anything *to do with this*.

My Anxiety Destroys Me Slowly

I know it's not the end of the world...

but my hair is falling out.
I'm ripping at my scalp.
My nails are bitten down.
I'm pulling layers of lip off
with my teeth and it tastes
like coppery missing.

 Like Alice and her "drink me,"
like you're gone for good

and I don't know how to keep
myself from shrinking.

Global Warming

Little lies like raindrops falling from your teeth,
washing words into gutters and cutting
like hail through our summer
of deceit.

But no liquid can
dim the halo of sunlight
cascading through your curls.
I remember every spot
that has ever gouged your bones
and I could place each mole
with my eyes tightly closed.
Still, I walk through life pretending
I don't know

how the left side of your lip
pulls tight when you're
not in control

and now it pulls when our
eyes meet in a crowd, when you find
me between bodies and lose me
in the swell

like you never meant to leave me,
but that's always how it goes,

we can't control the weather,
and the forecast
has been so

unpredictable.

calm in the dark

The Perfect Crime

This heart is covered in caution tape and barbed
wire. This heart is in a body bag. This heart....

I can't look at it,

can't understand why I murdered it with hands bare
and bloodied, nails like pocketknives, knuckles like
butterflies and I slice

at my own chest, I cut out the poison

until there is none left and I am a husk
of shredded skin, but I still reside in it—
there is nothing emerging from this mess
of molt.

There is what used to be and what is no more,
there is a special on late night television,
there is a crime scene and a perpetrator
they'll never apprehend.

Waters of Grief

When Alice said
"I do wish I hadn't cried so much,"
I can't relate.

I wish I cried more.
I wish I cried oceans.

When you left, I stood on my front porch and
watched you go. Silently. Slowly. There was no
grand goodbye scene. This was no movie.

Just you, walking to your car without a single
glance over your shoulder.

Just me, glossy eyed but not letting a single tear fall.

Those tears were too precious to waste on my steps.

I held those tears until they drowned me.

My ocean came much later. Months later. When I
realized you were so far gone there was no way to
catch you.

When I realized even crying oceans wouldn't soften
this blow.

calm in the dark

I cry so much now. I cry so much and I soak.

cat speranzini

calm in the dark

Trying Again

cat speranzini

calm in the dark

vii. introspection

Grief is the water I bathe in.
I let it soak into my skin
until the water is as cold as ice
and it's time to get out again…

Off With Her Head

These snakes had you in their sights,
their jaws open, ready to bite,
and if you looked at me just so
I might've let them have a go.

You deserve the same venom that you spat,
I was ready to Medusa your ass.

Yet, these unruly snakes wrap around
my forearm instead of your throat,
they remain coiled and dormant,
so Perseus has no beast to behead.
I let sleeping snakes lie instead.

calm in the dark

The Last Mermaid

The push and pull
of the rising tide
calls me into the deep
like a mermaid walking
on two feet

who has been on land so long
she forgot about the sea
and is only now remembering

she is the salt of the ocean,
the froth of the waves,
the sting of a man o' war,
the calm before
a hurricane.

Why I Stay Alive

I hold out for a mid-summer sunset,
the balmy seventy-five degrees with a breeze,
the humidity from the ocean hovering
in the air—tiny water droplets that cling
to my damp and tangled hair. I hold on
for cooling aloe over angry red sunburns.
I listen for the terns sailing past crashing
waves. I ride the undertow, let it drag me
down and set me free again. I bury my
pruned toes in the sand: an anchor
against the siren song of the deep.
I hold on for silence—an empty beach.
How easy it would be to get lost at sea.

calm in the dark

Island Time

The sun has never pierced me
as deeply as it did in Jost Van Dyke
when I was a young girl boldly
jumping into the glassy surface
of diamond-like brilliance
from the safety of our catamaran,
my body suspended in midair
for a second that lasted a year.
Every speck of sand, every drop of water
was crystal clear.
I caught the particles like butterflies
until I collided with the ocean.
Manta rays flew beside me,
their fins billowing into wings.
Turtles dove to the reef below,
barrel racing through coral.
Tomtate tickled my toes, my stomach,
the hairs on my too thin arms
as I swam to the off-bay bar
nestled in the shores of paradise.
My feet sank into burning sand,
my skin drank sunbeams
from the clear skies, blushing
as a precursor to becoming tan.
And I was so full of promise then,
I was part of the land

that spanned from beach to sea
and back again.

Growing

I am writing again.

I tell everyone he was my muse,
I pretend his presence added sunlight,
but it's his missing that fertilizes
the soil.

I mourned for him so beautifully
that my tears grew gardens
from his gone.

Doing the Work

My favorite game
is no longer chase, nor is it hide-and-seek.
I have stopped pursuing things that run
from me, I have stopped looking for what evades.
My hands can build castles if I bother
to shovel the sand.

I have stopped hoping it's sunny where you are.
Now, I keep the sunshine on my side of the beach,
now I build something
just for me.

Valkyrie

These wounds are self-inflicted—that is to say

everything I endure I create.
My skin is made of something stronger
than muscle and pus. I am exoskeleton and scales,
like a serpent biting its own tail or
the pounds of pressure exerted
by invertebrate claws
as if I am made to be
torn apart, split
open

and consumed, my life a test
of resolve, iron clad
arms built to carry
a sword,

a shield maiden
whose unbreakable will
deserves a warrior's death

on the battlefield.

The one where she saves herself

This water into wine trick isn't working—I don't want fermented sips of heaven like bottled stars flowing through parted lips. If I want to taste the sky, I'll look to it with eyes open and hair wild. I'll let the wind lift my wings off the ground and propel me to the stars themselves. I don't need bliss in a bottle, I need happiness as an aura of light radiating from my insides, blasting through the dark like a beacon until I am a lighthouse for lost girls. Girls with one shoe missing and one shoe on, girls who cannot find a prince or don't want to, girls who sing in attics to bluebirds, girls who are so exhausted they slumber in glass coffins, girls who wield their own weapons. I am stardust and sulphur: the princess left the castle with the dragon and they're off to find happily ever after.

calm in the dark

I heard them say you were chaos pt. II

and I believed them.
I used to write mountains about your goodness
as if convincing them might convince myself
and I still see how your curls catch the sunlight,
but it's not an eclipse—it's a cage. And I am
caught in your tangled vines, I am tied
to your countless lies. I let him slip through
my cracks like he was water and I a broken
vase, my breaks unlined—no gold for miles.
You called yourself Midas because all the
things you said turned to dust, everything you
touched burned up. The burning is nice,
it brought me to life, but I am not a phoenix,
I do not turn to ash and reappear. I crumble
into nothing, there is no one here.

In Case of Fire

The water is the safest place to be in case of a fire.
As a child, I was taught to wait at the dock if the
house burned down.

I've defaulted to those safety measures:
Use the dock as a meeting spot.

I left a piece of me there to wait for your return.
And wait. And wait some more.

If the water is the safest place to be when I'm on
fire, I will dip my singed feet in the sea.

You're not coming, but I finally extinguished the
flames.

I don't know what I expected from the one who
poured the gasoline.

calm in the dark

I Bind You, Nancy

Hello again, I'm writing you onto this page.
I am summoning you like a sorceress skilled
in necromancing.

These lines serve as a tether
from my body to yours, and though
you can't hear me, it's a comfort to talk
and pretend you'd listen to my words.

I left a part of me at the cabin in Maine,
I can't think about Portland without crying
and I'm not happy unless it rains.

The past is over with, you're never
giving me a reason for your wrongs
and it's okay, I forgive you

because I have no other option.
I spent so long placing blame,
but it never helped me move on.

I smile for pictures now. I let myself
relax. My hands aren't in fists,
I'm not bracing for an attack.

I summoned you here to tell you

that I will let you go. I summoned
you to say goodbye, a word
we never spoke.

I love you, I think that will always
be the case. Undeserved and
generous, it's more than you
gave. And that's okay.

I'm okay. You can't touch me
these days. That's my revenge:
your power is *gone*.

You have no sway.

calm in the dark

You Won't Like Me When I'm Down

There are pills for anxious minds,
pills for depression and suicide,
pills for psychosis, pills for impulse,
a pill for those intrusive thoughts
plaguing every waking moment.

Don't call me insane. I take my meds.
Nine little pills spaced out through the day so I can
function well enough to mask my Borderline traits.
And I'm fine, the doctor swears I'm alright
if I stay on a schedule like clockwork, like crazy
full planners and every minute accounted for
because if I deviate, I lose all progress
and I won't recover.

This is what healing looks like: color coded
and organized, don't suggest spontaneity
or I'll panic and find myself
back at the starting line.

And you won't like me when I'm down,
I'm an all or nothing kind of gal.

I'm Glad You're Here

Would you believe the mirror was kind today?
That I saw my reflection and didn't shy away.
That I didn't break the glass or turn off the light,
that I stood there and looked into my own eyes.
That I saw the tired soul and apologized.
She has been maiden and mother and one day,
I hope she lives to be the crone.
She's already beginning to wrinkle,
her breasts sag and her stomach hangs low,
but she stands tall and has a set to her jaw
and she fights fiercely for her cause.
She is flawed, she is human, she's not
a porcelain doll, but she's beautiful
and I love her and I'm lucky
to have the privilege of looking
at all.

calm in the dark

Fragility & The Nature of Death

She was soft and slipping, pollen painted
and wings flitting, all fluff and spindly legs
tumbling over herself until she was tangled
in the weeds and—

there is nothing, not a thing, holding her
back. Just stalks of grass brushing
and falling fast in the wind that spins her
wild until stomach is exposed and wings
collapse and I'm watching
her death.

It's an emergency room, it's a panic attack,
it's being cleared then expiring later that night
in the privacy of her bed.

And my son is crying
because a bee is dead.
And I am crying because
it's so easy to be alive one minute
and gone the next.

cat speranzini

Love is Knowing Whom to Choose
After Rupi Kaur

She asks me if I remember the one who got away,
the one I model love after, the one I've come to hate

and I do, I know who to credit with all of this
pain, this grief, this weight on my chest

but that is not love, it's not in his name,
losing myself in another and coming up empty,
love is something you gain.

The next time I choose love, I will choose
internally. I will start with my heart, no matter
how ruptured,

I will remember love is the power to give,
not the need to claim.

viii. introspection

No one else can fix the tangled vines
overgrown inside my head, but
you held my hand while I did it
and the darkest night seems brighter
with you in it.

cat speranzini

No Way

I have no way to thank you for staying
when you had every reason to go,
when I cried another man's name
in my sleep, when you held me in the throes
of all those bad dreams.

There's no way to thank you for forgiving
all the times I became the villain in your
story, all the times you were my knight
and I the dragon who tried to destroy you.

So if I am the siren and you are the sailor,
if I lured you to the depths of the sea
and stranded you in the middle of nowhere,
then I will swim you back to shore.

There is no way to thank you for
coming to aid me, but I can hold you
and tell you how much it means.

(*everything.*)

My Sky

I find you in the sun
embracing me with warm, golden rays,
breathing life into my winter worn skin.
You are the shine in my sky reminding me
there will be growth again.

I find you in the moon
caressing my cheek with luminescent light,
guiding me through the darkest night,
reflecting my inner fire when I forget
it's always burning inside.

Manta Rays

Did you know Manta Rays
can pass the mirror test?
That they mingle
with other species,
make friends, have
the largest brain to body ratio
of all the fish...

Sorry, I'm just
regurgitating facts.
This is all to say,
I didn't think anything
could surprise me these days,
but I met you
and everything
changed.

Better Days

There was no magical shift
in the fabric of the universe
more like a shift in my mind
and we still fight, but we try
to see the other side.
The dark lost its power
when I stopped relying
on outside light, I shine
from the inside and
everyone knows
like attracts like.

cat speranzini

Help it Bloom

Trapping chaos
in a bottle and admiring it—
like fireflies, like lightning—
is not love.

If you wrap
your arms around the void,
it does not hug you back.

It bites and consumes
and ravages, and the danger
is a thrill

but it is not love.

Watching a flower grow,
never plucking it from
the soil, never uprooting
something wild...

that is love.

Water the wild thing,
let the breeze ruffle its petals.
Allow its blossoming
under the sun.

calm in the dark

Never lock it away
in the house, never keep it
contained in shallow,
still water.

There is no container for love,
it is not a light to snuff out.

Love is alive.

(And we are meant to help it bloom.)

cat speranzini

The Memory

Someone told me water has memory
and I imagine every word I whispered
as condensation on your earlobe, I imagine
your kisses marked on my shoulder,
I imagine rain in the shape of your feet
on my floorboards.

I imagine the good wins over the bad,
I imagine I'm only a villain in my own head
and water knows the reason behind
why we do what we do, how the dark
contours our minds, and where the light
shines through.

If water remembers the moment we met,
would its shape be your smile
and my hand on my chest?

In Our Hips

Our hips can hold trauma
and they can also release it.
You sway your hips with mine,
spread my legs wide, hook
your foot around my ankle
and pull my frame open.
I grab your hips like they're
my confessional, I have done
bad things, *oh lord* I have
sinned, press me
into the mattress and
hold me for a minute long
stretch of skin to skin,
of your body against mine
until I can feel the trauma
releasing through my spine.

Spirituality

If there is a god
(which I don't believe there is, so we will use the
lowercase "g" to refer to this collective figment of
our imagination) then he never finished me.

There are no serotonin molecules in my whole
entire being and I don't know that I've ever been
happy.

I told my brother I don't like drugs because I want
to feel like myself and he said, "What? A dark
depressed mess?"

And I got angry, but maybe he makes a good point.
In any case, I'd rather be a mess than on
mushrooms.

Here I am, unfinished and missing some integral
parts. On drugs, but not the kind that mean you're
having fun.

I used to use men to fill the empty spots and when
that didn't work, I consumed wine like water. But I
am not the messiah and I am no whore. So
eventually I became addicted to words and now
there's endless sad prose about my disease.

calm in the dark

Anyway, if there's a god, he's not for me. I'd rather put my faith in the grass beneath my feet and the sanctity of someone else's body.

No Detour

This was all very sudden, there was no detour from the couch to the bedroom, from clicking locks to opening doors, from *my* house to *ours*.

Do you miss keeping secrets? Do you miss having something that's just yours?

Do You Love Me?

I have more inquiries than answers.
I ask him if he loves me a hundred times
a week and he usually says yes, but
sometimes he says nothing.
I wonder if he reconsiders
whenever I pose the question.

Recovery doesn't look like *happily ever after*,
it looks like waking up and deciding
to keep *fucking* trying.

A New Me

What if I always feel this way?
Like I am floating near my body, but never in it.
This was supposed to be temporary,
I thought the girl I used to be was still buried,
to be uncovered when I can find the strength to dig,
but what if she's not? What if this is the new me?
Is this what sensory deprivation feels like,
pitch black and floating?

I used to be terrified of the dark, of water without
a bottom.

Now when I float, I stop attempting to see. I keep
my eyes closed and relax my limbs, I stay light
and let go of the grief.

Buried Alive pt. II

About a year ago, I dug myself a grave.
Now, I'm digging myself free, clawing
my way out of this pile of memories.

Grief is so heavy.

I would have forgone burying myself
if I knew how much it weighed.

I Create

Bear witness to what has changed here,
a great and terrible shift in the wind.
This was the start of the universe,
the world could be anything
and I chose to craft it after your
eyes, I copied the laugh lines
and forehead crease, the peaks
and valleys of your face like
an altar to your image
that I will spend the
rest of my life
worshiping.

calm in the dark

We Won't Let it Fade

When our song plays, we listen to each and every word, hanging on them like a prayer into this unforgiving world. We won't let it fade, this devotion to each other. We won't let it fade as long as we're together. I carve you space with a pocketknife, you carve my initials into this life. And it's a good one, isn't it? It's as good as we make it. I'm glad you're here, I wouldn't want you to miss this. We won't let it fade, the way we both sing the same song. We won't let it fade, the tune carries on.

What Now?

When I was in high school,
I bought a shiny blue prom dress
that wrapped tight around my body.
My friend said I looked like a Greek Goddess.
Unique in my beauty.

I can only hope she meant Persephone:
goddess of blooming flowers and mortality.
I can only hope she meant my duality
makes me an anomaly.

I used to see unique as an insult.
Now, I prefer a crooked nose
and a gap between teeth.
I prefer wide hips
and strong thighs

like a bobcat on the hunt, all iron
and bone, like a ripened pomegranate
or the light calling you home.

Epilogue

Is the sunset as breathtaking on your side of town?
My side isn't scenic, no one visits on weekends,
but the sun sets like a star's final moments.
The colors could break you wide open.

I watch dusk bloom with
unmatched awe, like I'm witnessing
the birth of a new world.

I wouldn't trade this for calm waters
and strong fences. The chaos is critical
or I wouldn't think I deserve this.

It's a life worth living in spite of our struggles
because when daylight expires

the sun sets like shooting stars
and we make our wishes as they fall.

cat speranzini

Table of Contents

Prelude (12/23).. 13

Making the Bed... **15**

i. introspection 17

The North Star Misleads me in the Dark.......... 18

Buried Alive.. 19

Waves 20

Vampirical 21

Farewell.. 22

The Poem He'd Write About Me...................... 24

Silent Treatment... 25

Reveries 26

End of the World Party...................................... 27

Love In No Man's Land..................................... 28

Moon Time.. 30

Shipwrecked 31

Time of Death: 07.07.. 32

Bar Flies 33

Colossal 34

ii. introspection 35

I hope this message finds you well.................. 36

You Up?.. 38

White Chip 39

Haunting 40

This Heart is Out of Order................................41

Heartstrings 42

Talons 43

The Lovers Reversed................................44

Tidal 45

Metamorphosis................................46

Monster..47

Shark in the Water 48

Edge-runners................................49

Trauma Bond................................50

Overkill..52

Lying in It..55

iii. introspection 57

Playing the Victim................................58

Splitting..59

Don't Be..60

Rebirth 62

Quicksand..63

Doing Time 65

The River..66

A Necessary Evil 67

Keep Running 68

calm in the dark

The Cut That Never Closes.............................. 70

Stitches 71

Gentle.. 72

Selkie 73

Dreams / Nightmares...................................... 74

The Kraken... 75

iv. introspection 77

A Woman's Touch 78

Six Word Story... 80

Revisiting the Past 81

Loose Ends 83

Twin Flame... 84

Gaslight.. 85

Cool Girl 86

Lost at Sea... 88

Do it Anyway 90

Innocent Until Proven 91

Sheep in Wolf's Clothing 92

I Am Not.. 93

The Sins of Man in a Bar on a Monday........... 94

Writing an Ending... 95

***Getting Back Up*... 97**

v. introspection 99

cat speranzini

Love at Second Sight 100

Spilling Over 101

Lightning in a Bottle................................102

The Second Day 103

Eclipse 104

Savage...105

Opposites Attract 106

Tension 107

How To Hold Me.....................................109

If People Were Rain 110

Talking to Ghosts.....................................111

Tell me Something Awful...........................112

How Different am I *Really*? 114

Radical Acceptance..................................115

The Poem He'd Write About Me pt. II 117

vi. introspection 119

Headfirst 120

Inherited Rage 121

My Body is a Knife....................................122

Retrograde...123

What Color is a Thing that Leaves You? 124

Oceans 125

Rough All Over...126

calm in the dark

I am not always 127

Bad. Again 128

Beached.. 129

My Religion 131

My Anxiety Destroys Me Slowly 132

Global Warming 133

The Perfect Crime... 135

Waters of Grief... 136

Trying Again 139

vii. introspection.. 141

Off With Her Head.. 142

The Last Mermaid 143

Why I Stay Alive 144

Island Time... 145

Growing 147

Doing the Work 148

Valkryie.............. **Error! Bookmark not defined.**

The one where she saves herself................... 150

I heard them say you were chaos pt. II......... 151

In Case of Fire... 152

I Bind You, Nancy 153

You Won't Like Me When I'm Down 155

I'm Glad You're Here 156

cat speranzini

Fragility & The Nature of Death......................157

Love is Knowing Whom to Choose 158

viii. introspection...159

No Way 160

My Sky..161

Manta Rays...162

Better Days 163

Help it Bloom 164

The Memory..166

In Our Hips...167

Spirituality 168

No Detour 170

Do You Love Me? 171

A New Me 172

Buried Alive pt. II 173

I Create 174

We Won't Let it Fade 175

What Now? 176

Epilogue...177

Acknowledgements

In every mental health success story I've read, the conclusion is finding religion. In Dialectical Behavioral Therapy, having something to believe in is a key step to recovery. I grew up in a Catholic household and saw firsthand the downfalls of organized religion. God has never been my salvation. I find peace in the trees. I find it in the lake, I find it in the sun. I find it in the flowers. My salvation is the sky. The storms. The beauty of natural life. And it is these things I write about when I am in my darkest place. This collection was written over the course of four months. During that time, I went through too many evolutions to count. But there was one constant: the dark and my inability to sit in the stillness of the night. I sit in it now. I love the absence of light. The dark is where I shine.

cat speranzini

calm in the dark

ABOUT THE AUTHOR

Cat Speranzini was raised in New England in a picturesque town by the water. She attended Emerson College where she studied both poetry and fiction writing. Having struggled with mental illness her whole life, her writing focuses on difficult topics meant to help others navigate the chaotic waters of life. She is a reader for *Querencia Press* and the Editor-in-Chief of *Grey Coven Publishing*. Her poetry has been published by *Glass Gates Publishing*, *The Eunoia Review*, *Fuckus the Mag*, and *Querencia Press*. You can find Cat on her public Instagram account: @catsperanzini.poetry

cat speranzini

ABOUT THE AUTHOR

Cat Speranzini was raised in New England in a picturesque town by the water. She attended Emerson College where she studied both poetry and fiction writing. Having struggled with mental illness her whole life, her writing focuses on difficult topics meant to help others navigate the chaotic waters of life. She is a reader for *Querencia Press* and the Editor-in-Chief of *Grey Coven Publishing*. Her poetry has been published by *Glass Gates Publishing*, *The Eunoia Review*, *Fuckus the Mag*, and *Querencia Press*. You can find Cat on her public Instagram account: @catsperanzini.poetry

cat speranzini

Printed in the USA
CPSIA information can be obtained
at www.ICGtesting.com
CBHW060808070824
12786CB00020B/1109